# B·A·B·Y
# CRAFTS

Over 25 projects to make and give

# JULIET MOXLEY

EBURY PRESS
LONDON

*For my dear friend Sarah Charlesworth and her family*

First published in 1995

1 3 5 7 9 10 8 6 4 2

Text copyright © Juliet Moxley 1995
Photographs and illustrations copyright © Ebury Press 1995

First published in the United Kingdom in 1995 by Ebury Press
Random House, 20 Vauxhall Bridge Road, London SW1V 2SA

Random House Australia (Pty) Limited
20 Alfred Street, Milson's Point, Sydney,
New South Wales 2061, Australia

Random House New Zealand Limited
18 Poland Road, Glenfield
Auckland 10, New Zealand

Random House South Africa (Pty) Limited
PO Box 337, Bergvlei, South Africa

Random House UK Limited Reg. No. 954009

A CIP catalogue record for this book is available from the British Library.
ISBN 0 09 178692 4

Editor: Emma Callery
Design: Christine Wood
Photography: Marie-Louise Avery
Stylist: Gloria Nicol
Illustrations: Stephen Dew

Printed and bound in Portugal by Printer Portuguesa L.d.a.

# CONTENTS

# INTRODUCTION

*Nine years ago as the mother of two children I wrote my first book and called it* The Baby Kit. *In 1994, with 39 books under my belt - and another two children - I have written another book on the same theme. So here it is: the complete baby kit with instructions to show you how to make everything you need from those first items, moses basket lining and nappy stacker, to a knitted cardigan and hat and appliquéd bathrobe for the toddler.*

*Times change, but people go on having babies. When you have your first baby (and with many people subsequent ones), there is a great urge to create, or nest build. This book will help you do just that. The original book included patterns for items such as quilted baby boots which at the time were expensive. They can now be bought for a comparatively small amount of money and it would cost more to make them. So I have replaced the boots with other, more useful items, for today's parents. As well as taking things away, I have combined items so that, for example, a toy bag can also be a playmat and reversed with its PVC side uppermost it can be placed under a high chair at meal times. Painting smocks are decorated so they can be used as part of a dressing up game.*

*I have been very lucky in the talented designers who have helped me design and make up some of these new projects. I hope you like them and good luck with your baby!*

Juliet Moxley

# CHAPTER 1

# FIRST NEEDS

*A baby's first needs are small -
here you will find something to
meet all requirements: warmth,
cleanliness and safety.*

# MOSES BASKET

*Moses basket cribs are ideal for young babies; they look pretty and are light to carry. The baskets come in various shapes and sizes. All you have to do is line your basket and add a mattress, a cover and a quilt (see pages 14-15). The lining is easily detachable for washing. Instructions are given here for making a mattress. You may, however, decide to buy one.*

## MATERIALS

paper for patterns

3m (4yd) of 90cm (36in) wide quilted cotton fabric

fabric dyes (optional)

brightly coloured pompons (optional)

10cm (4in) velcro

sufficient bias binding for the circumference of the basket, 2cm (¾in) wide

60cm (2ft) of 1cm (½in) wide elastic

2.1m (7ft) narrow ribbon

1m (1¼yd) of 112cm (45in) wide waterproof fabric

1.2m (1⅓yd) of lightweight wadding

sufficient 5mm (¼in) wide elastic for the circumference of the base of the basket for each mattress cover

## TO MAKE THE PATTERNS

Before buying your fabric, make your pattern as you may find you need more fabric than suggested here if your basket is larger than average.

### Basket Lining

1 Stand your basket on a piece of paper and draw round the base. Cut out the shape and place it inside the basket. Press it firmly down into the bottom and, using a felt-tipped pen, draw a line round it just inside the edge to mark where the base of the basket joins the sides. This line will be your sewing line.

2 Measure the height of the basket at the highest point, add 10cm (4in) for the frill and 2cm (1in) for seam allowances. Measure the circumference of the basket double the length and add 2cm (1in) for seam allowances. Make a rectangular paper pattern of the dimensions you have just measured.

3 Cut an equilateral triangle pattern piece with each edge 15cm (6in) long.

4 Lay all the pattern pieces side by side to work out the amount of fabric that you will need. Remember to allow for 34 triangles pieces (to make 17 finished triangles).

If you are making matching quilt (see pages 14–15) and mattress covers, make the patterns for these at the same time and then check for fabric quantities.

### Mattress

The pattern that you cut for the base of the lining can also be used for the mattress.

### Mattress Cover

Put your mattress (either the paper pattern or the bought one) on top of the paper and draw round it. Lift up the mattress and add a further 10cm (4in) all round the shape you have just drawn. Cut round the outer line to make your pattern.

## MAKING UP

*Use 1cm (½in) seam allowances throughout.*

### Basket lining

1 To achieve the fabric effect in these photographs, we used gingham dyed various colours in a washing machine which we then pieced together to make a patchwork fabric. If you choose to do the same, dye the fabric and stitch the pieces together before cutting out.

2 Pin the pattern pieces on to the fabric and, with the exception of the triangles, cut one of each shape. Cut 34 triangles.

3 Stitch the short sides of the rectangle together, right sides facing. Using long running stitches, gather one of the long sides. With right sides facing, ease the gathered edge on to the edge of the base. Pin or baste in position and then machine.

4 Put the lining into the basket. If your basket is higher at one end than the other, trim the excess fabric at the lower end. Mark the position of the handles with pins on the basket lining. Cut the fabric between the pins and neaten the raw edges with bias binding. Sew short strips of velcro at the openings to close the gaps.

5 Make up each triangle by stitching two pieces together with right sides facing down two sides. Trim the seams and corners, turn right sides out and press flat. If you are using pompons, sew one on to one point of each triangle. Neaten the outside edge of the lining and sew on the triangles with the pompons hanging downwards.

6 On the wrong side of the lining and 7.5cm (3in) in from the outside edge, stitch both sides of the bias binding completely around the lining leaving a small gap to insert the elastic.

7 Insert the elastic into the casing and stitch the ends firmly together. Check the lining gathering is even around the basket.

8 On the wrong side of the basket lining, about 2cm (¾in) below the handle openings, sew a row of short pieces of ribbon, approximately 20cm (8in) long and 15cm (6in) apart, attaching them by their centres. Using an embroidery needle, push these through the basket and tie into bows on the outside. This will hold the lining in place.

### Mattress

1 Using the pattern cut for the base of the lining, cut three layers of wadding and two pieces of waterproof fabric. Baste the pieces of wadding together.

2 With right sides facing, sew the two pieces of plastic together. Leave a gap large enough to insert the wadding. Turn right sides out, insert wadding and close the gap by oversewing.

### Mattress Cover

1 Using the mattress cover pattern, cut as many covers as required. Turn under by 2mm (⅛in) all round to neaten.

2 Turn under again by 1.5cm (⅝in) leaving a small channel about 1.5cm (⅝in) wide. Thread the elastic through the channel.

3 Place over mattress and tie the ends of the elastic so that the cover is firmly, but not too tightly, attached.

# CRIB QUILT

*Here is a beautiful tiny quilt cover to match the moses basket on the previous pages. Make the quilt from matching or contrasting fabric to that of the moses basket lining. You can also make the quilt reversible by choosing a different pattern for the lining - two for the price of one.*

## MATERIALS

paper for pattern

2m (6½ft) of 90cm (36in) wide cotton fabric

fabric dyes (optional)

1m (1yd) of 90cm (36in) wide lining fabric

1m (1yd) lightweight wadding

3 pompons (optional)

## MAKING UP

1 To achieve the fabric effect in these photographs, we used gingham dyed various colours in a washing machine which we then pieced together to make a patchwork fabric. If you choose to do the same, dye the fabric and stitch the pieces together before cutting out.

2 Make a paper pattern using the crib base as a guide. Make the pattern slightly larger all round by 10cm (4in).

3 Using the pattern, cut one each of the following: top fabric, lining fabric, wadding. If your fabric is not quilted already, quilt the wadding on to the wrong side of the top fabric.

4 Make 3 triangles as you did for the basket lining (see page 11) and, making sure that the triangles face inwards, sew them along one short side of the quilt. You might decide to make the triangles from patchwork pieces like we did in the photograph opposite. With right sides facing, sew the lining fabric on to the top fabric round three sides. Trim the seam and corners, turn right sides out, press and close the opening by oversewing. Add pompons to the ends of the triangles.

# LAUNDRY BAG

*This is essentially a draw string bag. It is very capacious as babies seem to get through more washing than anyone else in the world. However, if the bag is rather on the large side for your needs, just scale down the dimensions and buy less fabric.*

## MATERIALS

2 x 77cm (30in) pieces of 90cm (36in) wide gingham in contrasting colours

---

fabric dye (optional)

---

fabric remnants

---

embroidery threads (various colours)

---

2m (2yd) ribbon or piping cord

## MAKING UP

*Use 1cm (½in) seam allowances throughout.*

1 To achieve the fabric effect in these photographs, we used gingham dyed various colours in a washing machine. If you choose to do the same, dye the fabric before cutting out.

2 From each large piece of fabric, cut out a piece measuring 77 x 86cm (30 x 34in). From the remnants, cut out 10 circles, 2 triangles, 2 oblongs and 2 semi-ovals each approximately 12cm (4¾in) across.

3 For the reverse appliqué, arrange the circles evenly on the bag front and back, with the right side of the cut-outs facing the wrong side of the large fabric rectangles (five on each). Pin and baste each circle about 3mm (⅛in) in from its edge.

4 On the right sides of the main fabrics and using very sharp, pointed embroidery scissors, cut away the top fabric from the centre of each circle within 6mm (¼in) of the basting stitches.

5 Snip into the edges of the circles and turn under by 3mm (⅛in). Baste the edges where they are turned under. Neaten with a hemming stitch and then carefully remove the basting. The result should be five circles of different coloured fabric showing through the top layer on both the front and back of the bag.

6 With right sides facing, sew the semi-ovals together along the circular edges; the triangles along two sides; and along three sides of the oblong. Trim the seams and corners, turn all the shapes right sides out and press flat.

7 With right sides facing, place the bag front and back together. Pin the sides and bottom together, sandwiching the unstitched edges of the semi-oval on one side, the oblong on another and the triangle on the third. Ensure they are facing inwards. Stitch the front and back together, trim the seams and corners and turn the bag right sides out and press flat.

8 Turn the top edge under by 5mm (¼in) and under again by 5cm (2in) and stitch leaving a gap at one side. This makes a casing for the ribbon or piping cord. Thread the cord through and pull to gather up.

# NAPPY STACKER

*Whether you use terry towelling nappies or disposable ones, you need somewhere to keep them. Why not make a jolly nappy stacker like this one?*

## MATERIALS

1 wooden coat hanger

paper for pattern

1.6m (64in) of 90cm (36in) wide fabric

fabric dyes (optional)

38 x 28cm (15 x 11in) piece thick cardboard

some brightly coloured pompons

## MAKING UP

*Use 1cm (½in) seam allowances throughout.*

1 Lay the hanger on the paper and draw around it, adding 1cm (½in) at the top and sides for seam allowances and 10cm (4in) at the bottom.

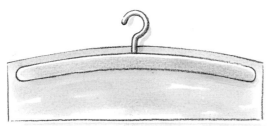

2 From the fabric cut: 2 pieces of fabric from the pattern piece; 14 equilateral triangles with sides each of 10.5cm (4in); 2 squares 60 x 60cm (24 x 24in); 2 rectangles 40 x 30cm (16 x 12in). (For details on making the dyed patchwork fabric see page 10.)

3 Take the coat hanger-shaped pieces of fabric and, with right sides facing, stitch around top and sides, leaving a 4cm (1½in) gap in the centre of the top, through which to thread the coat hanger. Turn edges under around the hole to neaten and stitch.

4 Stitch the triangles together in pairs (to make 7). Stitch with right sides facing and leaving a small gap along one edge to turn out. Trim seams and corners, turn right sides out, press and oversew the opening.

5 To make the bag, sew the two squares together along one side with right sides facing. Neaten the two outside edges and sew on the triangles, four on one side and three on the other so they alternate as in the illustration below.

6 With right sides facing, pin bag bottom to one of the rectangular pieces of fabric, leaving a front opening in the centre of one of the long sides of the base. Stitch together, turn right sides out and neaten the edge at the base opening.

7 Glue the cardboard into the centre of the wrong side of the other piece of rectangular fabric. Fold and stick the loose edges under and leave to dry. This will give a firm base to your nappy stacker.

8 Using a running stitch, gather around the top edge of the bag. Adjust the gathers evenly to fit inside the coat hanger sleeve. Pin, baste and machine into place.

9 Place card, fabric side up, in the base of the nappy stacker. Decorate the coat hanger sleeve with bright pompons.

# BABY SLEEPING BAG

*If you have ever suffered sleepless nights because your baby wakes up cold having lost blankets in the middle of the night you will love me for this pattern. This kind of sleeping bag has been used on the Continent for years but at the time of writing retails only in a very few shops in Britain and at a hefty price. It is an ideal way of keeping a baby warm while allowing her to kick and move around. After the baby is too big to sleep in the bag, you can open up the bottom seam and use it as a dressing gown.*

## MATERIALS

squared paper with a 5cm (2in) grid

1m (40in) of 112cm (45in) wide quilted fabric

3m (3⅓yd) of 13mm (½in) wide bias binding

61cm (24in) of 6mm (¼in) wide elastic

51cm (20in) closed end zip

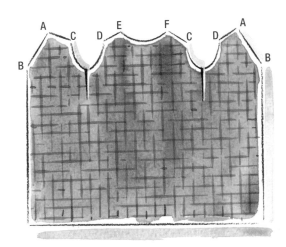

## MAKING UP

*Use 1cm (½in) seam allowances throughout.*

1 Draw the pattern given opposite on the squared paper.

2 Fold the quilted fabric in half with wrong sides facing. Place the pattern with the centre back on the fold and cut out the fabric. Do not cut along the fold line.

3 With right sides facing, sew both sets of darts and carefully press.

4 Open out the sleeping bag: it should look like the illustration above right. Sew bias binding round the raw front edges and the arm holes from C to D on both sides. Bind the neck from E to F.

5 With right sides facing, pin and stitch the shoulder seams (AC to DE and FC to DA).

6 On the wrong side of the bag, pin each end of the elastic into place as shown on the pattern so that it runs across the bag. Sew firmly in place using a running stitch.

7 Turn the bag the right way out. Place the left-hand centre front seam slightly over the right-hand centre front seam, overlapping by about the width of the binding. Sew up this seam for 30cm (12in) from the bottom of the bag (see illustration, below).

8 Using a zipper foot, insert zip from V-neck to top of seam you have just sewn.

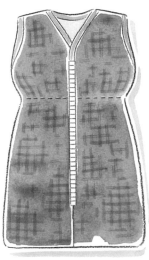

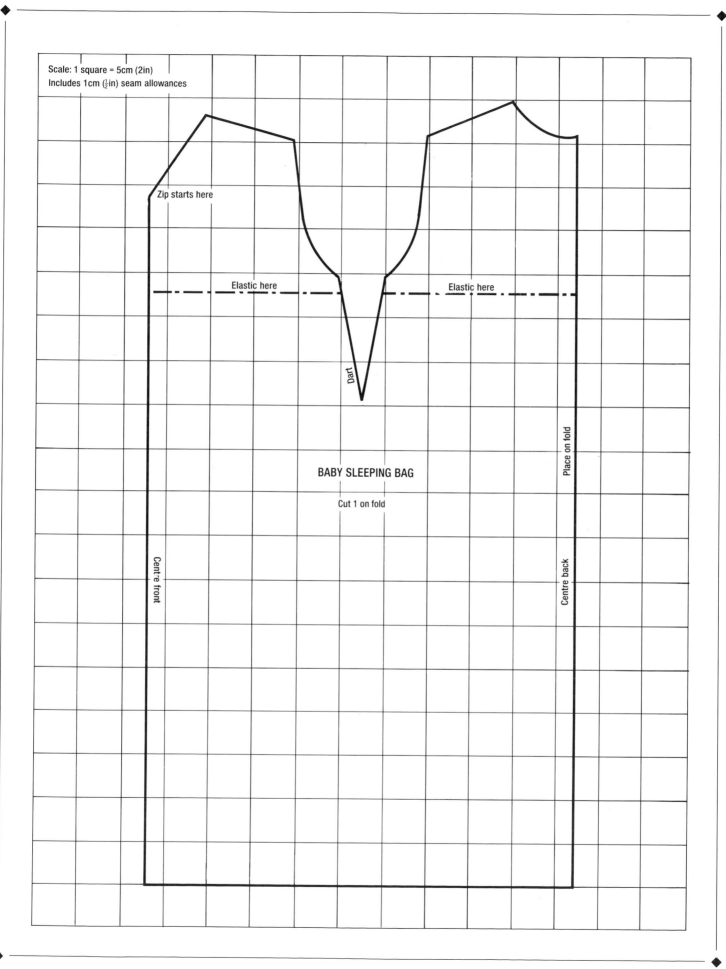

Scale: 1 square = 5cm (2in)
Includes 1cm (½in) seam allowances

Zip starts here

Elastic here          Elastic here

Dart

Place on fold

BABY SLEEPING BAG

Cut 1 on fold

Centre front

Centre back

**9** Neaten the bottom edge of the bag by overlocking or using a zigzag stitch. This will enable you to open up the bottom seam later on, so the bag may be used as a dressing gown when the baby has grown too big for the bag.

**10** Turn the bag inside out and, checking that the zip is in the centre front, stitch the bottom of the bag together (see illustration, below). Trim the seam and turn right sides out once more.

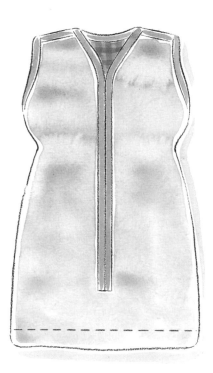

# TRAVEL SEAT

*Just because you now have a baby it doesn't mean that your friends' houses are baby or toddler proof. This travel seat enables you to take your baby with you for meals out, or with friends, restraining him safely and comfortably in any ordinary upright chair. The added advantage of this design is that the front of the seat covers the baby's body and doubles as a bib.*

Please note that this seat is not suitable for use in cars.

## MATERIALS

squared paper with 5cm (2in) grid

90cm (36in) of 115cm (46in) wide fabric, quilted on both sides OR 90cm (36in) of 115cm (46in) wide fabric, quilted on one side plus the same amount of lining fabric

1.8m (2yd) of 13mm (½in) wide bias binding

50cm (18in) contrast fabric

Fimo (various colours)

## MAKING UP

*Use 1cm (½in) seam allowances throughout.*

1 Draw the pattern given opposite on the squared paper. Add a 1cm (½in) seam allowance around each piece.

2 Fold the fabric in half, right sides facing, pin the pattern into place on the fabric and cut out the pieces. If using lining fabric, place the cut out pieces on the quilted pieces with wrong sides facing. Baste round the edges and treat each piece as an entity.

3 Fold the shoulder straps and loop piece in half lengthways, right sides facing. Stitch across one end and down the long edge of each piece. Trim the seams and corners, turn right sides out, press and oversew the remaining end.

4 Sew the loop in place on the right side of the main piece, as marked on the pattern.

5 Fold the seat, with right sides facing, along the fold line marked on the pattern. Stitch the side seams together. Trim and turn right sides out.

6 Sew bias binding around the curved edges of the seat and the raw edge of the back.

7 With right sides facing, sew each tie to the short ends of the waistband. If you should choose to add some reverse appliqué to the waistband as in the photograph overleaf now is the time to do it. Follow the instructions for reverse appliqué as given on page 16, but instead of circles, make square holes.

8 Fold the complete tie in half lengthways with right sides facing and stitch the ends and long edge, leaving the waistband open. Trim the seams and corners, turn right sides out and press, turning under the seam allowances on both sides of the waistband.

9 Place the raw edges of the seat into the waistband and firmly oversew into place. Sew the shoulder straps into place (as illustrated, opposite).

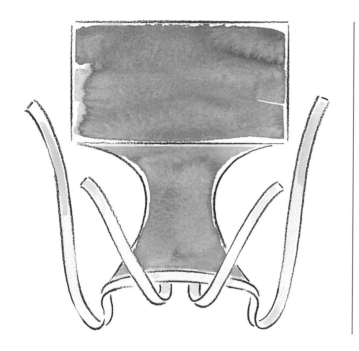

**10** An appliqué pocket has been attached to the front of this travel seat. See *The Princess and the Pea* wall hanging on pages 70–3 for making instructions and refer to the picture overleaf for adding the details.

**11** To use the travel seat slip the main body of the seat over the back of a chair. Sit the baby on the chair and pull the shaped piece of the seat up between his legs. Tie the waistband around the back of the chair and pull up the shoulder straps. Thread them through the loop at the back and tie securely.

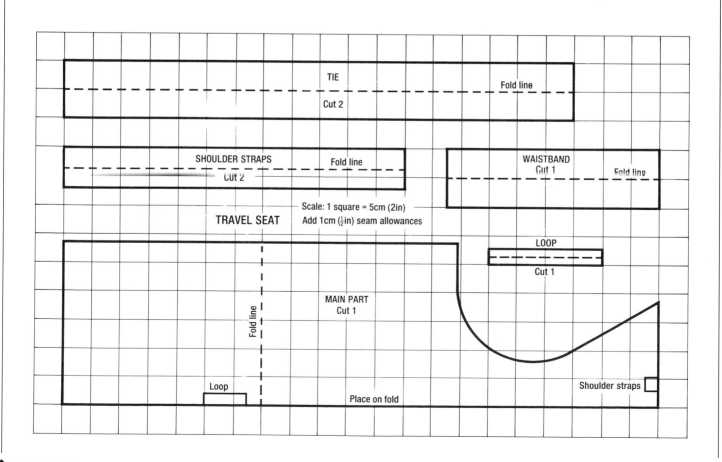

TIE
Fold line
Cut 2

SHOULDER STRAPS
Fold line
Cut 2

WAISTBAND
Cut 1
Fold line

Scale: 1 square = 5cm (2in)
Add 1cm (½in) seam allowances

**TRAVEL SEAT**

LOOP
Cut 1

Fold line

MAIN PART
Cut 1

Loop

Place on fold

Shoulder straps

# DECORATED NIGHT DRESSES

*Here are two ways of decorating a night dress. If you can't buy a plain one, make one and then decorate it. The red night dress featured here is decorated in reverse appliqué circles. The white one is mainly decorated with back stitch embroidery but the hems are outlined in different coloured embroidery threads which are anchored into position using contrasting colours.*

*Like the night dresses, the caps are made from white and red winceyette and the balls on the ends are made by the same method as the ball on the mobile on page 78.*

---

### MATERIALS

night dress(es) to decorate

*For Red Night Dress*

fabric remnants

embroidery threads (various colours)

*For White Night Dress*

tailor's chalk

embroidery threads (various colours)

size 22 embroidery needle

remnant green fabric

cotton wool

---

## MAKING UP

### The Red Night Dress

**1** Baste 7.5cm (3in) circles of fabric all over the inside of the night dress, with right sides of the circles facing the wrong side of the night dress.

**2** Using very sharp, pointed embroidery scissors, cut away the top layer 6mm (¼in) within the basting lines to reveal the fabric below. Fold back by 3mm (⅛in) and neaten with stab stitches. Remove the basting stitches.

**3** Embroider a decorative border around neckline as described in Step 2 to the right.

### The White Night Dress

**1** Using tailor's chalk, draw the design or words you are going to embroider directly on to the night dress. The words are written in a wavy line around the edge of the garment and each word is worked in a contrast colour to the word next to it.

**2** Lay one colour thread along the border of the sleeve. Thread the needle with a contrast colour and using over stitches work along the seam over the first colour, catching it into place. Repeat for the other sleeve, the neck and hem line.

**3** Using back stitch, sew over the words you have written in tailor's chalk. This night dress has the following words and embroidered decorations:

*Sleeve 1:* my cuddly teddy bear – 3 french knots – sleepy

*Sleeve 2:* 4 french knots - hot chocolate pillows and sheets

*Neck line:* my teddy bear – 5 french knots – pillows and sheets – 5 french knots – cosy hot water bottle dreaming sleeping

*Hem:* a drink of hot chocolate – 5 french knots – dreams my teddy bear – 8 french knots – dreaming whilst sleeping of clouds and flowers – 4 french knots – cosy in bed with my hot water bottle – 5 french knots.

**4** Write and then back stitch words around the hat, too. Here we have: Wee Willie Winkie runs through the town upstairs and downstairs in his night gown.

# RAG DOLL PYJAMAS CASE

*This rag doll pyjamas case is a real doll complete with a wardrobe of petticoat, dress, shoes and neckerchief. Under her skirt is a bag closed with ties at the back into which you put the pyjamas.*

## MATERIALS

*For Rag Doll*

squared paper with a 2.5cm (1in) grid

1m (1yd) natural coloured calico

20cm (8in) of 90cm (36in) wide white knitted cotton fabric

kapok

wool

felt scraps (pink, blue and black)

50cm (20in) of 90cm (36in) wide yellow gingham

two 22 x 5cm (8½ x 2in) strips leather or fabric

15cm (6in) gold cord

*For Petticoat*

30cm (12in) of 90cm (36in) wide white cotton

75cm (30in) narrow lace

30cm (12in) narrow elastic

*For Dress*

50cm (20in) of 90cm (36in) wide yellow gingham

20cm (8in) of 90cm (36in) wide yellow polycotton

1m (1yd) lace

1m (1yd) velvet ribbon

1m (1yd) satin ribbon

ribbon rosebuds

buttons

## TO MAKE THE RAG DOLL

*Use 1cm (½in) seam allowances throughout.*

1 Draw the pattern given opposite on the squared paper.

2 Cut four arms, four legs, and two upper body pieces from the calico. Cut two head sections from the knitted cotton.

3 With right sides facing, sew the two head pieces together leaving a gap at the neck and also sew together the two pairs of arms and legs leaving a gap at one end of each for filling. Trim the seams and corners and turn right sides out. Fill each piece with stuffing and oversew the gap at the neck on the head.

4 Make the hair by winding the wool round a piece of card and cutting both sides. The width of the card should be the length of the hair measured from the centre top of the head. Lay the wool in a strip on top of the head and sew down around the top of the head to make a fringe.

5 Add the features to the face. Make the nose by running a small circle of stitches and gently gathering them up. The eyes and mouth are small circles of felt.

6 With the right sides of the two upper body sections facing each other, sandwich each arm between the body front and back and sew into position, as illustrated below. Turn right sides out. Put the body and legs to one side.

## TO MAKE THE PYJAMAS BAG

**1** Cut the lower body pieces from the calico and the gingham (the lining).

**2** With right sides facing, sew the two back pieces of calico together, 4cm (1½in) down from the top and 4cm (1½in) up from the bottom leaving a gap in the centre to make the back opening. Repeat for the gingham lining. Turn under seams at openings and press.

**3** Make six 25cm (10in) long ties from ribbon or gingham fabric by cutting strips measuring 27 x 5cm (11 x 2in), and folding them in half lengthwise with right sides facing. Stitch along one short edge and the long edge, turn right sides out, press and oversew the remaining short edge to close gap.

**4** With wrong sides facing, place the calico back piece on top of the lining back piece, sandwiching three ties on either side of the centre back opening. Pin and baste in place. Top stitch close to the edge through all layers at the centre back. Baste together the outside seams and treat as one piece.

**5** Take front piece of calico and pin and baste pleats at top and bottom edges. Repeat for the gingham lining. Baste the calico and gingham layers together with the wrong sides facing along the sides seams and then treat as one piece.

**6** With right sides facing, stitch together front to back along side seams only. Press seams open.

**7** Place the upper body (with arms) inside the lower body bag, right sides facing. Pin together and stitch through all layers twice for strength. Turn right sides out.

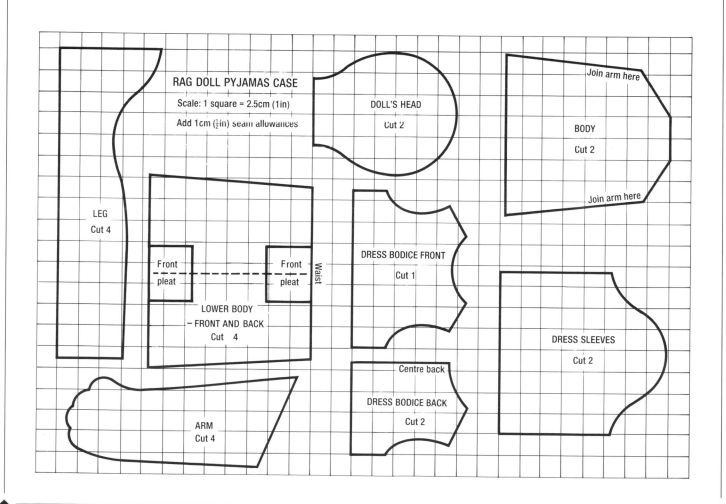

RAG DOLL PYJAMAS CASE

Scale: 1 square = 2.5cm (1in)

Add 1cm (½in) seam allowances

DOLL'S HEAD
Cut 2

Join arm here

BODY
Cut 2

Join arm here

LEG
Cut 4

Front pleat    Front pleat    Waist

LOWER BODY
– FRONT AND BACK
Cut 4

DRESS BODICE FRONT
Cut 1

DRESS SLEEVES
Cut 2

Centre back

DRESS BODICE BACK
Cut 2

ARM
Cut 4

**8** Fold up seam allowance for bottom of bag and baste a piece of lace all round this edge. Insert top edges of legs between bottom edges of bag. Top stitch through all layers. Remove basting.

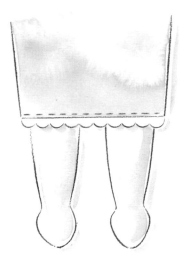

**9** To make the shoes, fold each strip of leather or fabric in half lengthways right sides facing. Stitch along the long edge and trim the seam allowance. Turn right sides out, place on doll's feet, fold up front over toes and cross the corner over the front. Stitch securely in place by hand. Sew a gold cord bow at side fronts.

**10** Fill the body with stuffing. Place head on body and turn all raw edges in and oversew by hand.

## TO MAKE THE CLOTHES

### Petticoat

**1** Cut one piece of fabric to measure 25 x 75cm (10 x 30in).

**2** Sew the narrow lace along one long edge of the fabric to neaten.

**3** With right sides facing, sew the short sides together to form a tube. Turn under the top edge and stitch in place and then insert a length of elastic to fit the doll's waist.

### Dress

**1** Using the pattern pieces cut out with the doll's body, cut:
◆ two sleeves from the gingham
◆ two bodice fronts and backs from the yellow lining.
◆ In addition, cut a piece of gingham measuring 34 x 80cm (13½ x 31½in) for the skirt.

**2** With right sides facing, sew front and back of bodice together at the shoulders. Repeat for lining. Press seams open.

**3** Make three button loops from gingham. With right sides facing, sew outer bodice and lining bodice together along top edge and centre backs, sandwiching two rouleau loops between right centre backs. Trim seams and corners, turn right sides out and press.

**4** Sew a running stitch round top of the sleeves and pull up gathers to fit the armholes. Adjust gathers to fit and sew into place. Trim seams and turn right sides out. Sew ribbons on to sleeves and pleat and decorate with ribbon rosebuds.

**5** With right sides facing, sew along the sleeve and bodice seams.

**6** Decorate one long edge of the skirt with lace, velvet ribbon and satin ribbon. With right sides facing, fold the skirt in half to form a tube. Sew three-quarters of the way up the short side. Neaten the edge and press open the seams.

**7** Run a line of running stitches around the top of the skirt and pull up to form gathers. Arrange neatly, pinning skirt to bodice with right sides facing. Sew together.

**8** Make a sash from velvet ribbon. Stitch in place at the back with an extra rouleau at the waistline. Sew on the buttons, matching the positions of the rouleau loops.

**9** Add a ribbon rosebud at the top of the bodice.

**10** Make a scarf from a triangle of the gingham edged with narrow lace.

# BATHROBE WITH HOOD

*Bathrobes with hoods are so much nicer than those without as they can be snuggled into before bedtime, and are a great way to play peek-a-boo!*

---

## MATERIALS

squared paper with a 5cm (2in) grid

1.9m (2yd) of 148cm (60in) wide towelling OR 2.6m (3yd) of 90cm (36in) wide towelling

remnants brightly coloured cotton fabrics

60cm (¾yd) of 13mm (½in) wide bias binding

---

## MAKING UP

*Use 1cm (½in) seam allowances throughout.*
*All seams should be finished by turning under or using a zigzag stitch.*

1 Draw the pattern given opposite on to the squared paper. Ensure you are using the right size pattern and add a 1cm (½in) seam allowance around each piece.

2 Pin the pattern on the towelling and cut out. Cut the star fish, shell and fish motifs opposite out of the cotton remnants.

3 With right sides facing, sew the two belt sections together along the narrow seam. Fold in half lengthways again with right sides facing and stitch along one narrow end and the long edge. Turn the belt right sides out, press and oversew the open end to close it.

4 With right sides facing, sew the fronts to the back at the shoulders. Neaten edges and press seams open.

5 With right sides facing, stitch the sleeves to the armhole openings. Neaten edges and press seams towards sleeves.

6 For each belt loop, cut a piece of material 10 x 5cm (4 x 2in). Fold in half lengthways, right sides facing. Stitch along the length, trim the seam and turn right sides out. Baste each end of the loop on to the dots marked on the pattern for the front ensuring that it lies towards the garment.

7 With right sides facing, pin the side and sleeve seams together and stitch. Neaten the edges and clip along the under-arm curves. Press seams open.

8 Stitch the body and sleeve hems by turning the fabric under twice and top stitching 1cm (½in) from the edge.

9 With right sides facing, stitch the rounded sides of the hood together. Neaten the edges, clip the curves and press seam open.

10 With right sides facing, stitch the hood to the robe at the neck edge. Keeping the seam together, neaten the seam with bias binding. Press towards the robe.

11 Join the centre seam of the facing band and turn in one side of the band by 1cm (½in) and press. Pin the right side of the opposite long edge of the band to the wrong side of the garment so that the band runs up one front edge, around the hood and back down the other front edge. Stitch in place leaving the seam allowance at either end (at hem line) unstitched. With the seam facing towards the band, turn up the seam allowance of the band at the hem edge and stitch in place. Turn the band to the right side of the garment, so that the pressed edge is under the band. Baste, and top stitch all edges of the band, 6mm (¼in) in from the edge.

12 Pin the motifs around the bottom of the bathrobe and one or two on the hood. Sew with a line of running stitches. Go over the line with a close set zigzag stitch to neaten.

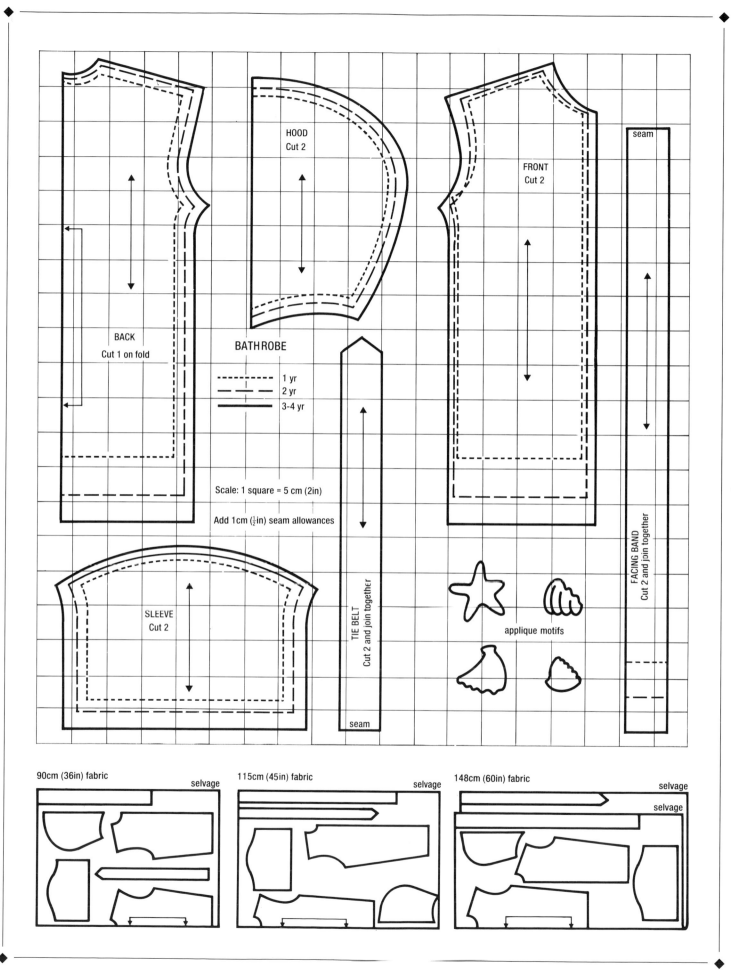

HOOD
Cut 2

seam

FRONT
Cut 2

BACK
Cut 1 on fold

BATHROBE

- - - - - 1 yr
— — — 2 yr
———— 3-4 yr

Scale: 1 square = 5 cm (2in)

Add 1cm (½in) seam allowances

SLEEVE
Cut 2

TIE BELT
Cut 2 and join together

seam

applique motifs

FACING BAND
Cut 2 and join togethter

90cm (36in) fabric                    selvage

115cm (45in) fabric                    selvage

148cm (60in) fabric                    selvage

selvage

# BERET AND CARDIGAN

*Some children look much better in strong and/or dark colours than they do in pale ones. This cardigan and beret are knitted in dark colours with bright contrasting bobbles. However, the same design can be made up in any colours you desire.*

## MATERIALS

4 x 50gm balls of DK wool in main colour (black)

1 x 50gm ball each of 4 contrasting colours of DK wool (these can be made up of oddments of wool and more than four colours may be used if desired)

1 pair each of 3¾mm (No 9/US 6) and 4mm (No 8/US 5) knitting needles

1 stitch holder

5 coloured buttons

## ABBREVIATIONS

alt = alternate; beg = beginning; cont = continue; dec = decrease; inc = increase; K = knit; mb = make bobble, each in a different colour yarn ([K1, P1, K1, P1] all into next stitch, turn, K4, turn, K4, turn, K2 tog twice, turn, K2 tog); P = purl; rem = remain(ing); rep = repeat; st(s) = stitch(es); st.st = stocking stitch; tog = together.

## TO MAKE THE BERET

With 3¾mm (No 9/US 6) needles, cast on 78 sts in contrast colour.
Rib K1, P1 for 2 rows.
Change to main colour and cont for another 5 rows in rib.
**Next row** P3, (inc once purlwise in each of next 2 sts, P1, inc purlwise in next st, P1) 14 times, inc once purlwise in each of next 2 sts, P3 (122 sts).

Work 6 rows in st.st.
Change to 4mm (No 8/US 5) needles and K 2 rows in contrast colour. Return to main colour.
Work 2 rows in st.st.
**Next row** (K9, mb) 12 times, K2.
Work 5 rows in st.st.
**Next row** K4, mb, (K9, mb) 10 times, K to end.
Continue to make bobbles every 6th row, alternating positions as above, working pattern as follows.
Work 3 rows in st.st.
**Shape crown**
**1st row** K2 tog, K to end (121 sts).
**2nd row** P.
**3rd row** (K13, K2 tog) 8 times, K1.
**4th row** P.
**5th row** (K12, K2 tog) 8 times, K1.
**6th row** P.
**7th row** (K11, K2 tog) 8 times, K1.
**8th row** P.
**9th row** (K10, K2 tog) 8 times, K1.
Cont in st.st dec on every alt row as before until the row (K1, K2 tog) 8 times, K1 has been worked.
**Next row** P.
**Next row** (K2 tog) 8 times, K1.
Run end through remaining sts and fasten securely.

## TO MAKE THE CARDIGAN

### Back
With 3¾mm (No 9/US 6) needles, cast on 64 sts.
Rib K1, P1 for 5cm (2in).
**Next row** Inc 11 sts evenly across row (75 sts).
Change to 4mm (No 8/US 5) needles and work

in st.st for 4 rows.
**Next row** K7, (mb, K9) 6 times, mb, K7.
Work 5 rows in st.st.
**Next row** K2, (mb, K9) 7 times, mb, K2.
Work 5 rows in st.st.
Rep the last 12 rows until the work measures 38cm (15in), ending with a wrong side row.
**Shape sholders**
Cast off 11 sts at beg of next 4 rows.

## Left Front

With 3¾mm (No 9/US 6) needles, cast on 32 sts.
Rib K1, P1 for 5cm (2in).
**Next row** Inc 5 sts evenly across row (37 sts).
Change to 4mm (No 8/US 5) needles and work in st.st for 4 rows.
**Next row** K3, (mb, K9) 3 times, mb, K3.
Work 5 rows in st.st.
**Next row** K8, (mb, K9) 2 times, mb, K8.
Cont until work measures 35cm (13½in), ending with a wrong side row.
**Shape neck**
Cast off 6, K to end (31 sts).
**Next row** P29, P2 tog.
K2 tog at neck edge of every row until 22 sts remain.
Cont till work measures the same as Back.
**Shape shoulder**
Cast off 11 sts at shoulder edge.
Work 1 row.
Cast off remaining 11 sts.

## Right Front

With 3¾mm (No 9/US 6) needles, cast on 32 sts.
Rib K1, P1 for 5cm (2in).
**Next row** Inc 5 sts evenly across row (37 sts).
Change to 4mm (No 8/US 5) needles and work in st.st for 3 rows starting with a P row.
Cont as for Left Front, reversing neck and shoulder shapings.

## Sleeves

With 3¾mm (No 9/US 6) needles, cast on 36 sts.
Rib K1, P1 for 5cm (2in).
**Next row** Inc 4 sts evenly across row (40 sts).

Change to 4mm (No 8/US 5) needles and work in st.st for 4 rows.
**Next row** Inc in first st, K4, (mb, K9) 3 times, K4, inc in last st (42 sts).
Work 5 rows in st.st.
**Next row** K1, (mb, K9) 4 times, K1.
**Next row** Inc in first st, P40, inc in last st.
Keeping pattern correct, inc 1 st at each end of every following 7th row until 54 sts are on the needle.
Without further shaping but keeping the pattern, work until sleeves measure 29cm (11½in).
Cast off.

## Collar

With 3¾mm (No 9/US 6) needles and right side of work facing, pick up and K 22 sts from Right Front, 15 sts from back of neck, K2 tog, rem 14 sts from back of neck, 22 sts from Left Front (74 sts).
Work in K1, P1 rib for 5 rows.
Change to 4mm (No 8/US 5) needles and cont in rib until collar measures 9cm (3½in).
Finish with two contrasting colours of your choice, working 2 rows of each colour.
Cast off loosely in rib.

## Front Bands

With 3¾mm (No 9/US 6) needles, cast on 8 sts.
Rib K1, P1 until band reaches up front when slightly stretched.
Cast off in rib.
Mark 5 positions for buttons.
Work another band the same length making button holes to match markers thus:
(K1, P1) twice, wool forward, K2 tog, K1, P1.

## To Make Up

For the beret, sew back seams together.
For the cardigan, join shoulder seams.
Sew on sleeves placing centre of sleeves to shoulder seams.
Join side and sleeve seams.
Sew on front bands with button hole band on right side.
Sew on buttons.

# PLAYMAT/CATCHPATCH

*This mat is wonderfully versatile. You can simply use it as a playmat. Or by pulling up the draw string threaded around the edge, you can gather up the toys in it and hang them up out of the way. Or lay it under a high chair, plastic side up, and catch the crumbs as they fall. It's great, too, for using outside, especially for picnics.*

## MATERIALS

1.1m (45in) of 112cm (45in) wide plasticized fabric

1.1m (45in) of 112cm (45in) wide cotton or polycotton fabric

1.1m (44in) of lightweight wadding (optional)

small pieces of textured materials and ribbons

PVA glue

black fabric felt-tipped pen

pieces of sticky-backed fabric (various colours)

1.6m (64in) cotton tape

3.75m (4¼yd) narrow tape or piping cord

## MAKING UP

1 Take the plasticized fabric, fold it in quarters and draw a quarter circle using a piece of string and a pencil. Cut through all four thicknesses, open out and you have a circle. Use this circle as a pattern to cut the cotton fabric and wadding, if you are using it.

2 Working on the cotton fabric, cut out the shapes for the fields, river, railway and roads as shown in the photograph opposite. Pin, then glue or baste, the fabric pieces on to the background cloth. Using a running stitch, sew the pieces in place and then either sateen stitch or zigzag over the line of running stitches.

3 Repeat Step 2 but this time putting the houses, shops, church and station, road markings and railway tracks in place.

4 Using the fabric felt-tipped pen draw in details such as windows, doors and words, for example 'school'.

5 Next work on the PVC back of the mat. Using the small photograph overleaf as a guide, cut out shapes from the sticky-backed plastic and stick them on to the mat.

6 Stick the base of the design down first and slowly build up the design. Vary the design of your houses. Some can have two floors, others three. Doors can be square or have rounded tops. Add fish of various colours and size to the pond on the other side of the road.

7 Cut the cotton tape into eight lengths of 20cm (8in) and fold over to make loops. Sew them on to the right side of the cotton mat at equal intervals round the edge ensuring they are facing inwards.

8 With right sides facing, pin the plastic mat to the cotton one. Machine round the edge, leaving a gap just large enough to turn through. If you are using wadding, insert it now; it may need trimming to fit.

9 Trim the seams, turn the mat right sides out and oversew the opening to close it. Top stitch right around the edge to give a neat finish.

10 Thread the narrow tape or cord through the loops and tie the ends.

# PAINTING SMOCKS

*More than just simple painting smocks, these can double up as bibs, overalls, aprons and even dressing-up clothes. Just choose your theme and decorate. They are made from wipe-down PVC and decorated with sticky-backed plasticized material which comes in plain colours, a variety of patterns, or clear.*

*The two smocks shown here are an artist's smock complete with paint brush, paint blobs and palette, and a cowboy with neckerchief, sheriff's badge, belt and the top of the jeans showing. Other themes could be a spaceman, alien, princess, fairy, Robin Hood, animals such as a cat, cow, pig or bird - or whatever the latest craze happens to be.*

## MATERIALS

squared paper with a 5cm (2in) grid

50cm (20in) of 112cm (45in) wide sticky-backed plastic

1.4m (1½yd) cotton tape or ribbon

pieces of sticky-backed fabric (various colours)

## MAKING UP

1 Draw the pattern given opposite on to the squared paper (seam allowances are included).

2 Pin the pattern on to the plasticized fabric and cut out two pieces.

3 With right sides facing, join the shoulder seams.

4 Turn under all raw edges and sew with a running stitch.

5 Cut the tape into four equal lengths to make the ties.

6 Measure up 21cm (8½in) from the bottom edge of the smock and sew a tape to each side edge at this point.

7 Using a biro, draw the shapes to decorate the smock on the back of the sticky-backed plastics.

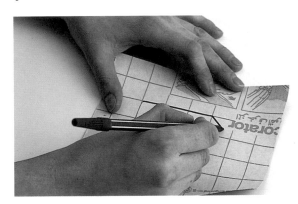

8 Cut each shape out. Remove the backing paper from the background shapes first and stick them on to the smock. Slowly build up the picture by removing the backing paper from the details and sticking these on to the background shapes.

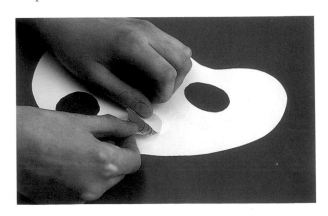

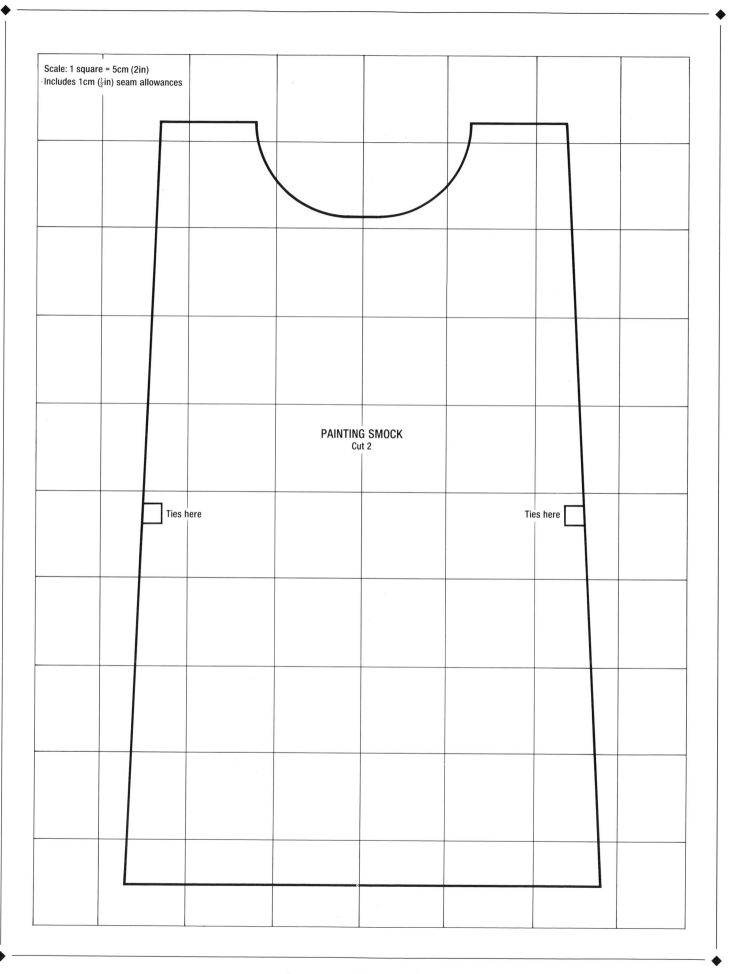

Scale: 1 square = 5cm (2in)
Includes 1cm ($\frac{1}{2}$in) seam allowances

PAINTING SMOCK
Cut 2

Ties here

Ties here

# CRAZY PATCHWORK TEDDY

*This delightful bear is made from pieces of patchwork and stuffed with kapok. As you will see, a traditional bear takes on a completely new look when made from fabric. For ease of making, the bear has sewn, rather than jointed, limbs which means that he is not suitable for very young children to play with but is ideal as a decorative gift to sit on a shelf. You can make him larger or smaller by reducing or enlarging the pattern on a photocopier.*

## MATERIALS

squared paper with a 5cm (2in) grid

70cm (¾yd) of 114cm (45in) wide calico

remnants of fabric

embroidery thread to match or contrast with the fabric scraps

2 teddy eyes and fixings, OR buttons

## MAKING UP

*Use 1cm (½in) seam allowances throughout.*

1 Draw the pattern given opposite on the squared paper.

2 Cut out the pattern pieces, pin on to the calico and cut out.

3 To make the patchwork fabric, cut pieces of material to fit on to the calico pattern pieces. Stitch them down so that no raw edges show where materials overlap. The pieces can be all different shapes and sizes (this is crazy patchwork). Embroider with french knots, feather stitch, chain stitch or simple cross stitch.

4 With right sides facing, make two pairs of ears by stitching along the outer curves. Clip into the curves and turn right sides out. Stuff lightly.

Turn under the lower edge of each ear, and stitch the front to the back. Make a small pleat at the bottom front edge of each ear.

5 With right sides facing, stitch the darts in the two head pieces as indicated. Then stitch the front seams together (again with right sides facing) up as far as the nose. Stitch the head gusset between the two sides of the head as shown in the illustration, below.

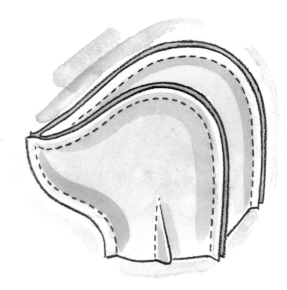

6 Turn the head right sides out and insert or sew on the eyes. Turn under the neck by 5mm (¼in) along the bottom seam and baste. Stuff the head firmly and oversew the neck seam to close. Remove the basting.

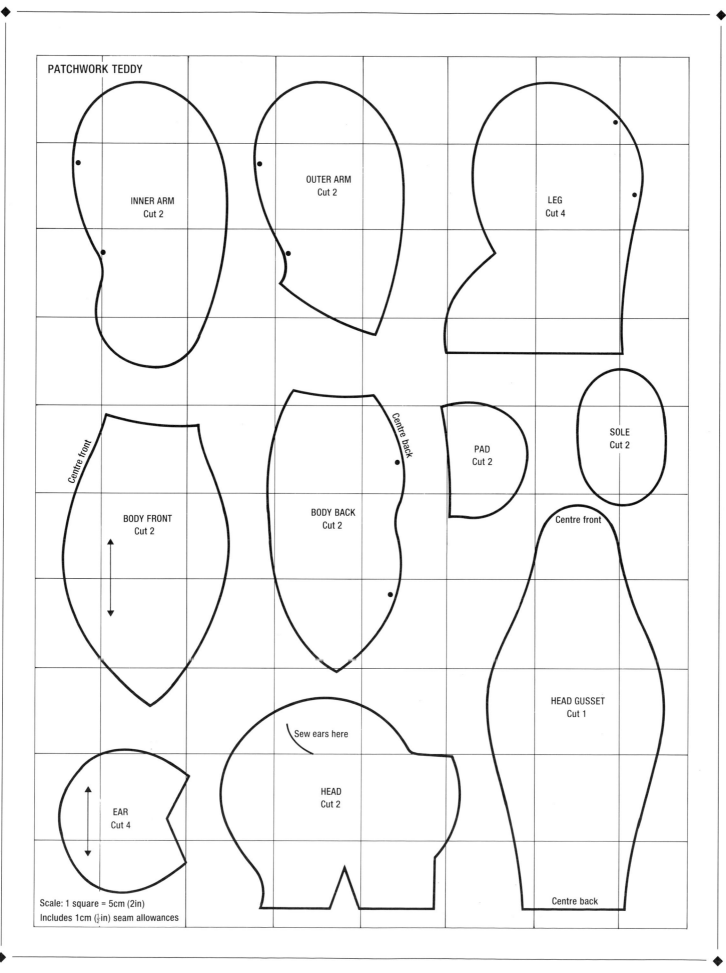

PATCHWORK TEDDY

INNER ARM
Cut 2

OUTER ARM
Cut 2

LEG
Cut 4

Centre front

BODY FRONT
Cut 2

Centre back

BODY BACK
Cut 2

PAD
Cut 2

SOLE
Cut 2

Centre front

HEAD GUSSET
Cut 1

Sew ears here

EAR
Cut 4

HEAD
Cut 2

Centre back

Scale: 1 square = 5cm (2in)
Includes 1cm ($\frac{1}{2}$in) seam allowances

**7** Slip stitch the ears on to the head as marked in the pattern.

**8** With right sides facing, stitch the body fronts together along the centre. Stitch the body backs together, leaving a 10cm (4in) opening seam between the dots. Stitch the front to the back, including the neck edge. Turn right sides out.

**9** Stitch the pads to the inner arm with right sides facing. Again with right sides facing, stitch the inner arms (complete with pads) to the outer arms leaving a gap as indicated between the dots for stuffing.

**10** With right sides facing, stitch the legs together to make two pairs. Stitch down the two outside seams leaving a gap as indicated between the dots. Stitch the soles to the bottom of the legs. Turn the legs right sides out.

**11** Stuff the arms and the legs and close the gaps with overstitching. Using slip stitch, sew them on to the body firmly, as illustrated below left.

**12** Stuff the body firmly and sew up the back seam opening.

**13** Pin the head to the body and then sew it firmly into place using slip stitch.

**14** Using three strands of embroidery thread, sew the nose and mouth on to the face, as illustrated below.

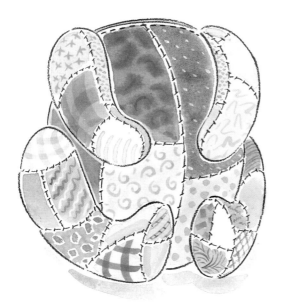

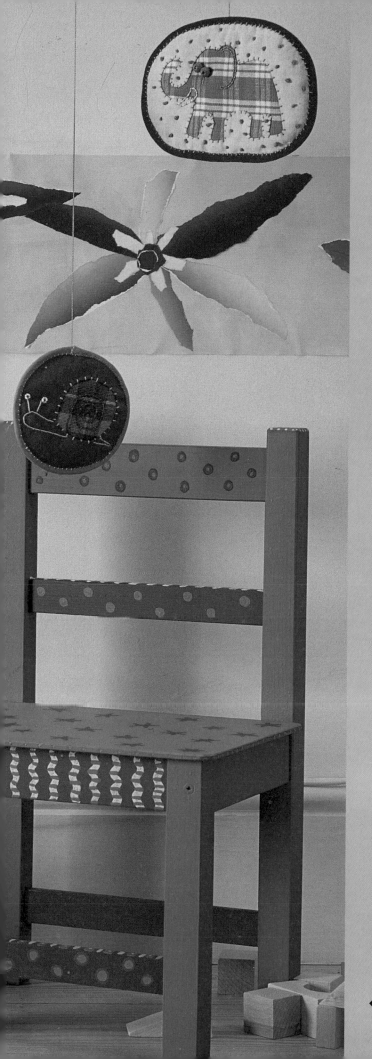

# CHAPTER 3

# THE NURSERY

*Decorating the nursery is great fun. Here you can find ideas for a frieze, a painted toy box and chair, a matching cot and quilt cover, an animal mobile and a wondrous wall hanging depicting the fairy tale of the princess and the pea.*

# TORN PAPER FRIEZE

*Specially designed nursery friezes can be quite expensive and although you can make a frieze from cut paper shapes, torn paper has an appeal of its own. You can buy plain border paper so that you can design and make your own border or buy lining paper and cut it to the depth you desire. The background paper may be painted with emulsion, as may ordinary sugar or cartridge paper which may then be used for tearing to create the frieze.*

*Any paper which is not too tough may be torn. It is worth experimenting before you start making your frieze to find out where the grain of the paper is and so which direction is easier to tear. There are such a variety of papers available today it is hard to know where to begin. There are coloured papers, some with matt surfaces, others with shiny or laminated surfaces. Some coloured papers even come ready-gummed. Then there are tinted, polished, metallic and multi-coloured papers. Beware tissue and crepe papers, however, for although these give interesting textures, they are probably too flimsy to use for a wall frieze.*

## MATERIALS

background paper (lining paper or plain border paper)

---

emulsion paint

---

paint brush

---

rough paper

---

papers to tear

---

wallpaper paste or glue pen

---

Blue Tac

## MAKING UP

**1** If you are using lining paper, cut it to size and then paint the background colour on to the border. Leave to dry.

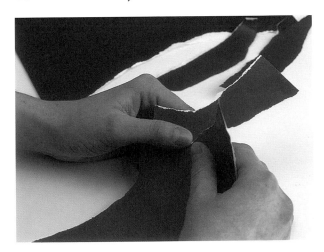

**2** Draw your design on to rough paper. Remember that when you tear paper it will not come out exactly as you have drawn it. The drawing will help with composition.

**3** There are two main methods of tearing paper. The first is just done directly, and the

other is to fold the paper and then tear it along the folds. Folding paper helps to make symmetrical shapes. Here we chose to tear the paper to achieve a wonderful free design (see photograph, opposite).

4 Remember that a shape may be built up from many torn elements. So, for example, the separate petals in a flower or a horse chestnut leaf may be made from many pieces of torn paper. Add these details on top of the main elements of the design, building up to the finished effect layer by layer (see photograph below).

5 When you have torn enough shapes, start arranging them on the background. Once you are pleased with the composition, Blue Tac the pieces to stop them moving.

6 Mix a small bowlful of wallpaper paste according to the manufacturer's instructions or use a glue pen. Remove the Blue Tac from each piece of paper before finally sticking it on to the background. Leave the whole composition to dry before sticking the frieze on to the wall.

# PAINTED TOY BOX AND CHAIR

*The painted toy box and chair seen here are unusual for painted furniture in that you really do not need to be good at art or painting to achieve such bright and lively finishes. You may paint on natural wood or wood which has already had a background colour painted on to it. Some paint shops will mix small quantities of emulsion for you and some manufacturers mix small pots of paint for trial runs but these are usually in pastel shades: you might prefer to mix your own colours.*

*When you are preparing the wood for painting, always overfill any cracks and holes with filler as it will shrink slightly. If the crack or hole is quite deep, apply the filler in two or three coats, allowing it to dry between each application. Use glasspaper wrapped around a block of wood when finally smoothing the surface.*

## MATERIALS

| |
|---|
| toy box |
| chair |
| glasspaper |
| white spirit |
| acrylic, satinwood or emulsion paints |
| paint brushes - a broad one for background colours and artist's ones for patterns |
| plates for mixing paint colours |
| masking tape (optional) |
| matt polyurethane varnish |

## PAINTING THE TOY BOX

1 Fill any holes on the box with wood filler. Leave to dry and then rub down the surface with the glasspaper.

2 Brush and then clean the surface of the wood with a cloth dampened with white spirit to remove any grease or dirt.

3 Apply the background colour(s). The reason the box look so jolly is that we chose contrasting background colours for the sides of the box, the lid and the rim. Our background colours were blue, mauve, green, and purple.

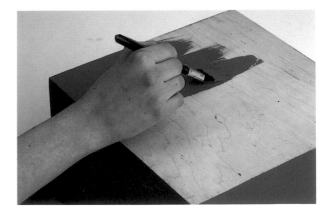

4 You might choose to apply the background colours in stripes. Stick strips of masking tape over the areas you wish to paint in this way to make good clean lines and to prevent one colour from seeping into another.

**5** The patterns here are are made up of overlapping lines, circles, dots, stars and squiggles. Either draw the patterns on in soft pencil first or, if you are confident, paint them on freehand.

**6** Paint details over the basic patterns. Here we added pink lines and orange dots. If you don't like a pattern, wait for it to dry and then just go over it with some more background colour. Wait for the background colour to dry and then reapply the pattern.

**7** As toy boxes come in for a great deal of wear and tear, cover them with a coat of matt polyurethane varnish.

## PAINTING THE CHAIR

**1** Prepare the wood as for the toy box and ensure it is quite clean before painting it.

**2** Paint the background colours. To reflect the variation in background colours on the toy box, we chose to use different colours on the chair legs, seat, back and cross braces.

**3** Decorate the chair as you did for the toy box. As there are so many different areas on the chair you might decide to use a greater variation of decorative devices. Some ideas are given below and on the photograph overleaf.

**4** Cover the chair with a coat or two of polyurethane varnish to prevent paint from chipping off.

### SOME DECORATIVE SUGGESTIONS

stripes on narrow edges and around the box lid

stripes with dots added to all the stripes of one colour

circles with dots and sunbursts

circles with contrasting rims

add dots and circles to contrasting rims

crosses decorated with dots

stars with contrasting dots on the points

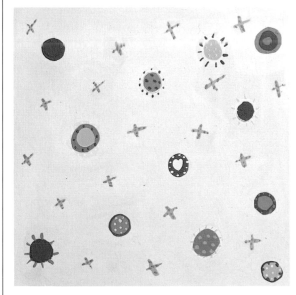

# THE PRINCESS AND THE PEA WALL HANGING

*This hanging is made using appliqué, reverse appliqué and various different embroidery techniques. It measures 118 x 38cm (46 x 15in) and is hung by loops from a piece of dowelling. It depicts the old fairy story of the princess and the pea and incorporates lots of visual surprises inside the pockets, and under the flap at the top of the hanging. It is decorated with buttons made from Fimo.*

## MATERIALS

This hanging can be made up of any fabric remnants you have to hand but you will also need the following materials:

Fimo (various colours)

two 121 x 41cm (47½ x 16½in) pieces cotton fabric

embroidery threads in lots of colours

three 21 x 32cm (8¼ x 12½in) pieces cotton fabric

1m (40in) of 13mm (½in) wide bias binding

30cm (12in) ricrac braid

few small beads

121 x 41cm (47½ x 16½in) piece lightweight wadding

## MAKING UP

### The Buttons

1 Following the manufacturer's instructions, mix some Fimo colours together, roll into small balls and press flat so that you have 1.5cm (¾in) diameter discs. Make 22 buttons for the hanging. They do not all have to be circular and you can add details, such as a line or a dot to the buttons, to add interest.

2 Using a skewer, make two holes in each disc to make holes for stitching in place.

3 Bake in the oven at the temperature suggested by the manufacturer.

### The Back of the Hanging

1 Cut nine small remnants in different patterns, each approximately 8cm (3in) square. Scatter them with their right sides down on to the wrong side of one of the large pieces of fabric and pin and then baste them near their edges.

2 On the right side of the main fabric, draw shapes such as circles, diamonds, hearts, spirals, crosses, and triangles within the basting lines.

3 Using very sharp, pointed embroidery scissors, cut within the pencil marks through the main fabric only and then turn under the edges where you have cut away and neaten using

an embroidery thread and stab stitches. Remove the basting. This is the reverse appliqué technique which is used to cover much of this wall hanging.

4 Sew four buttons, evenly spaced, at the top of the hanging.

## The Pockets

Each pocket is made of at least 7 strips of varying widths taken from remnants; some are as narrow as 1cm (½in) and made up from bias binding - the finished effect should look like random thickness mattresses. The following instructions are for a sample pocket, you may choose to use different dimensions:

1 Cut the following strips from remnants, adding approximately 5mm (¼in) for seam allowances:
   ◆ two 5 x 33cm (2 x 13in)
   ◆ four 7 x 33cm (2½ x 13in)
   ◆ four thin strips which together make up 7 x 33cm (2½ x 13in)

2 Take one of the 21 x 32cm (8¼ x 12½in) pocket linings and place the two 5cm (2in) wide strips on top of one another at the top of the piece. Turn under the bottom edge and neaten with stab stitches. Below this piece, please the thin strips of fabric in single layers and neaten these in the same way, but at both the top and bottom. Below this add the two 7cm (2½in) strips, each of two thicknesses, and neaten these at the top and bottom. You should now have an outer pocket made up of neat - but uneven - stripes.

3 On the double thicknesses of cloth, draw out shapes (as you did on the back of the hanging). We used triangles, squares, hearts and oblongs. Cut and neaten these to reveal the fabric beneath. Be careful to cut through only one layer of cloth and not the lining of the pocket as well.

4 Either use bias binding or cut and neaten a piece of bias fabric and use this to neaten the top edge of the pocket.

5 Repeat Steps 1 to 4 for each of the other two pockets.

## The Princess and the Bed

As you may remember from the fairy story, the princess slept in a very deep bed with many mattresses.

1 To make the bed posts, cut two long narrow strips from remnants, each 2.5 x 118cm (1 x 46in) and stitch them down the sides of the front of the hanging about 2.5cm (1in) in from the edge. Neaten with stab stitches.

2 Cut three pieces of fabric 3 x 35cm (1¼ x 13½in) from remnants. Sew these on to the hanging horizontally, 15cm (6in) down from the top of the bed posts. Turn under all the edges and neaten with stab stitches. These are the first of the princess's mattresses.

3 Cut a head and pyjamas, a pillow and head rest and sew on top of the three horizontal pieces of fabric. With a running stitch, embroider the princess's features, hands and hair. Then decorate the pyjamas with rows of running stitch, and embroider her feet with concentric circles (see photograph on page 71).

4 Cut a quilt cover of three layers, each with one straight and one wavy edge. Sandwich them together and decorate the top two layers using reverse appliqué. Attach the quilt on to the top of the hanging by the straight edge so that it covers the princess.

5 Neaten the quilt edges by turning under. Neaten the wavy edge of the quilt and decorate with some ricrac braid. Sew four button holes along the bottom.

6 Mark where the buttons should be with a pin and then sew them on to the front of the hanging so the quilt may be fastened down to hide the body of the princess.

## The Pockets and Embroidery

1 Below the three lines of mattress, embroider a row of spiders.

2 Stitch on the first pocket so that it just covers the spiders, turning under all the edges.

**3** Make another three mattress strips as above and sew them into position. Sew five buttons on the middle mattress.

**4** Below these three strips, embroider two white mice with pink tails.

**5** Repeat Steps 2 and 3 above to attach the next pocket.

**6** Below the three strips, embroider the following articles lost by the princess – comb, brush, crown, ball, slippers.

**7** Add the last pocket so that it covers these things as in Step 2 above.

**8** Cut a double layer of material from remnants measuring 7 x 36cm (2½ x 14in) and work reverse appliqué to look like springs. Stitch the strip to the hanging beneath the mattresses.

**9** Embroider a stump work pea, cut away the material below and pad the pea with cotton wool to make a firm green pea.

**10** Embroider flowers beneath the mattress in a random design.

## The Straps for Hanging

**1** Cut eight strips from remnants, each measuring 6 x 25cm (2⅓ x 9½in). Make four straps by stitching the strips together in pairs, right sides facing and making a 1cm (½in) seam allowance. Turn right sides out and turn in the ends to neaten. Edge with strips of bias binding held in place with stab stitches.

**2** Sew a button hole 1cm (½in) in from each end on each strap.

## Finishing the Hanging

**1** Sandwich the wadding between the front and back fabrics. Baste together and then sew bias strips all around the hanging to neaten.

**2** Sew a row of four buttons on the top front to mirror those on the top back.

**3** Attach the four loops to these and hang over a piece of dowelling. Hang on the wall.

# DECORATED COT AND QUILT COVER

*Decorating your baby's cot is a really lovely way to personalize it. The easiest way to do it is to put the cot together without its bottom and then to stand inside it and paint and climb out to paint the outside. In this way you can easily see it from all angles.*

*Before beginning to paint any furniture that a baby might chew, check that the paint is lead free and conforms to all health and safety regulations. In fact, most modern paints do, and it is when repainting old cots that you should be most careful in case the existing paint contains lead!*

*This quilt cover is easily adapted to fit an average sized pram, crib, cot or single bed. It is decorated using waterproof fabric pens and paint which can be applied before or after the quilt is made up.*

## MATERIALS

*For Cot*

wood filler

glasspaper

turpentine

natural sea sponge

emulsion paints (petrol blue, white, aquamarine, purple, pink, orange, yellow, lime, mauve)

artist's brushes (various sizes)

clear matt polyurethane varnish

*For Quilt Cover*

tape of half the longest dimension of the quilt cover OR make ties from any excess fabric

50cm (½yd) tape with stud fasteners

felt-tipped pen

masking tape

tailor's chalk  or a soft pencil

felt-tipped pens or paints

fabric paints (optional)

---

*Fabric quantities for Quilt Cover*

For a crib (70 x 70cm [28 x 28in]):
75cm (30in) of 228cm (91in) wide fabric OR
1.5m (60in) of 90cm (36in) wide fabric

For a cot (100 x 120cm [39 x 47in]):
1.25m (50in) of 228cm (91in) wide fabric

For a single bed (135 x 200cm [53 x 78in]):
2.9m (3⅓yd) of 228cm (91in) wide fabric

## DECORATING THE COT

**1** Repair any parts of the cot that need mending making sure there are no sharp or rusty pieces which may be reached by a small child. If any filling is needed, do this with a wood filler.

**2** Rub the filler and surface down with fine glasspaper, brush off the dust and wipe with a rag dipped in turpentine.

**3** Using the sponge, apply petrol blue to either end of the cot.

**4** Mix the white with aquamarine and, using a broad brush, paint on top of the sponged colour. This will give a watery feel to the background.

**5** Repeat Steps 3 and 4 for the bars of the cot on both inside and outside edges.

**6** Using a soft pencil, draw the fish shown in the photograph below at either end of the cot. Paint the body of the fish purple and leave to dry.

**7** Mix pink with purple and paint on the tail, fins and spots. Paint deeper pink wavy lines on the tail and orange lines on the fins.

**8** Add pink scales and paint the face orange with a pink mouth.

**9** Paint the fish eye with the same mixed pink and purple used on the fins. Add a deep purple circle around the eye and yellow in the centre of the body spots.

**10** Using yellow mixed with lime, paint wavy seaweed lines up the bars of the cot and round the fish.

**11** Using orange, paint small starfish randomly over the bars on the outside of the cot and round the fish. When they are dry, paint them with small yellow dots.

**12** Draw a symmetrical sea wave pattern on the base of the cot where the bars join on to it. Paint this in a petrol blue/white mixture and then dot with petrol blue.

**13** As a finishing touch, paint a small turquoise square at the end of the cot. Paint an orange starfish on top of this and surround the square with a thin purple line dotted with mauve.

**14** When all the paint is dry apply a protective coat of clear matt polyurethane varnish.

## MAKING THE QUILT COVER

**1** Fold the fabric in half, right sides facing, so that it is approximately the size needed. Add a 1cm (½in) seam allowance all round and cut away any excess fabric.

**2** Open out and neaten the edges by turning under each side by 5mm (¼in) and then again by the same amount and stitching in place.

**3** Fold in half with right sides facing and sew along the top and bottom edges. Sew a quarter of the way up the side from the bottom edge and a quarter way down the side from the top edge. Close the remaining gap by either sewing on ties or a strip of tape with stud fasteners attached.

# DECORATING THE QUILT COVER

**1** Draw your design on to paper using a thick felt-tipped pen. Place it under the top of the quilt cover with newspaper beneath the design to protect the rest of the cover and the work surface. Keep in place with masking tape.

**2** Using tailor's chalk or a soft pencil go over the design on to the cover. If you cannot see the design through the fabric take out the design and make the lines heavier. Or cut out a template and draw round this on to the cover.

**3** Go over the outline of the design using fabric felt-tipped pens and then colour in the design with other colours or paints.

**4** If using fabric paint, wait for this to dry and then turn the cover inside out. Place newspaper between the top and bottom of the cover and iron to fix. Remove the paper and turn the cover right sides out.

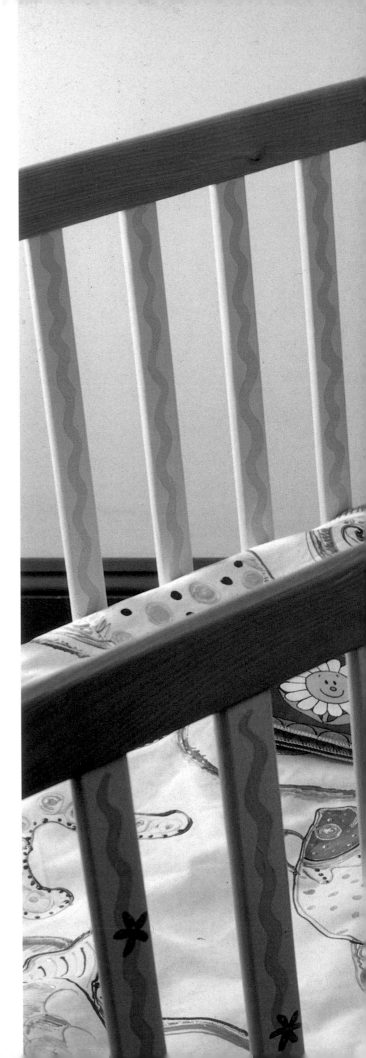

# ANIMAL MOBILE

*One of the first things a baby does is to focus on strong colour. It is therefore a good idea to hang an interesting mobile using simple shapes and bright colours over her moses basket or cot to look at. This one is made using reverse appliqué which involves sandwiching layers of fabric together and then cutting away different parts to reveal the layer below.*

*There are five pieces on this mobile and a soft cotton ball hangs from the central shape. The whole mobile is most easily hung by crossing two metal coat hangers together and hanging the pieces from each corner and one from the place where the hangers cross.*

## MATERIALS

fabric remnants

20cm (8in) lightweight wadding

50cm (20in) of 13mm (½in) wide bias binding (5 colours)

embroidery threads (4 colours)

10 wooden beads (various colours)

4 small plastic yellow beads

1 cotton wool ball

2 metal coat hangers

## MAKING UP

1 For each mobile piece cut two plain and two patterned pieces of fabric and one of wadding to the same size. We chose two ovals, two circles and one smaller circle for the middle.

2 Pin each mobile piece together as follows: one plain fabric on the bottom with a piece of patterned fabric on top of it, both facing downwards; a piece of wadding in the centre; another piece of patterned fabric, this time facing upwards, and a plain one on top. The plain and patterned fabrics can be swapped over as long as the wadding is in the centre.

3 Baste the pieces together around the edge and then neaten each edge by covering the basting

stitches with bias binding sewn on using embroidery thread in a contrast colour.

4 With a soft pencil, outline a motif of your choice on each mobile piece on both the top and bottom layers. We used a different one for each piece: elephant, tortoise, bird, snail and a small circle. Keep the shapes fairly simple as they will then be easier to work.

5 Using very sharp, pointed embroidery scissors carefully cut away from the centre of the shape you have just drawn to reveal the layer of fabric beneath the top one. Cut away to within 6mm (¼in) of the pencil line.

6 Very carefully fold under the raw edges and stitch down using a contrasting colour embroidery thread. The shape of the motif should now be clearly defined. Carefully remove the basting stitches.

7 Repeat Steps 5 and 6 for the other side and each of the other mobile pieces. Then sew on beads for eyes (the wooden beads for the elephant, tortoise and bird; the plastic beads for the snail) and embroider features such as ears, tusks, feet, beak or markings using a variety of stitches. Add

french knots to give a lovely textural contrast to the flat fabric.

8 To make a small ball to hang below the central motif, cut two small circles of cotton fabric. Sew one to the other three-quarters of the way around. Stuff very firmly with cotton wool until it is a tight ball and oversew the opening to close. Sew concentric circles on the underside of the ball and hang from the smallest motif by an 8cm (3in) long embroidery thread.

9 Attach embroidery thread to the top of each of the other motifs so they are about 75cm (30in) long. Hang the motifs from crossed coat hangers as described in the introduction above and if necessary adjust the lengths of the threads in order to balance the mobile.

# CHAPTER 4

# SPECIAL OCCASIONS

*With the arrival of a baby come other special occasions such as the Christening and birthdays. Celebrate the birth with a uniquely decorated pin cushion or a cross stitch sampler, celebrate the first birthday with a personalized plate, and enchant your child with tales of Father Christmas, hanging a special stocking over the fireplace.*

# CHRISTENING ROBE

*The birth of a new baby is a wonderful event in a family, and a Christening not only welcomes the child into the church it is also a time for friends and family to get together to welcome the new baby. In the past, Christening robes have been handed down from one generation to the next. You may be lucky enough to have inherited a family Christening robe, as the one here which was made by my great-great-grandmother. If not, we have worked out the pattern for you.*

*As babies have delicate, sensitive skins, remember to use the softest, finest fabrics possible. Use a fine cotton lawn, but if you are going to embroider on the cotton you may need to use two thicknesses or back it with a lightweight interlining.*

*As a final touch, booties can be customized. Small satin boots are available in many baby shops. Remove any superfluous bows or trims and then sew on your own lace and embroider them. Remember to use narrow lace on small boots so that they are not overwhelmed.*

## MATERIALS

squared paper with a 5cm (2in) grid

1.5m (60in) of 115cm (46in) wide cotton or cotton lawn

15 x 12cm (6 x 5in) lace for centre front panel

2.4m (2⅔yd) of 4cm (1½in) wide lace

2.85m (3yd) of 1cm (½in) wide broderie anglaise

2.85m (3yd) of 6cm (2½in) wide broderie anglaise

34cm (13½in) scalloped lace

1.05m (42in) of 1.5cm (⅝in) wide bias binding

1m (40in) of 1.5cm (⅝in) wide fine lace

2.85m (3yd) of 1cm (½in) wide ribbon

2.4m (2⅔yd) of 7mm (⅜in) wide ivory ribbon

## MAKING UP

*Use 1cm (½in) seam allowances throughout.*

1 Draw the pattern given opposite on the squared paper. Add a seam allowance of 1cm (½in) around each pattern piece.

2 Lay on the fabric which should be folded in half, right sides facing. Cut out all the pieces.

## Skirt

1 Using tailor's chalk or basting stitches, mark the positions of the pleats all the way across each of the skirt panels. Pin and stitch ensuring that the pleats are parallel to one another. Press the pleats down.

2 Sew the pleated panels and 4cm (1½in) wide lace together so that there is a lace insert between each pleated panel (see illustration, below).

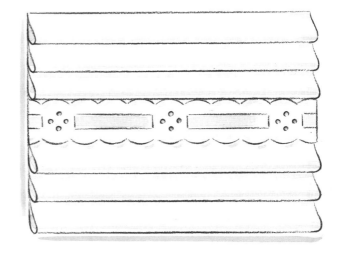

**3** Sew the 1cm (½in) wide broderie anglaise on top of the 6cm (2½in) wide broderie anglaise (see illustration, right). With right sides facing, sew the lace you have just prepared on to the side edges and the bottom of the pleated front panel. Make sure that it is gathered well round the bottom corners so that it lies flat.

**4** With right sides facing, sew left and right backs together at the centre back, from the bottom up to the notch. At the centre back opening, press along the 2.5cm (1in) fold line on the left-hand side to the wrong side, and secure with a line of horizontal stitches.

**5** Sew the remaining prepared lace to the bottom of the skirt back.

**6** With right sides facing, sew front to back at the side seams, being careful that the lace on the skirt front is caught in evenly.

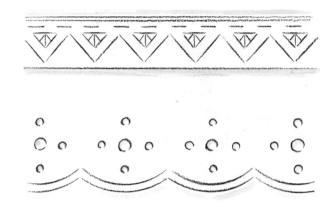

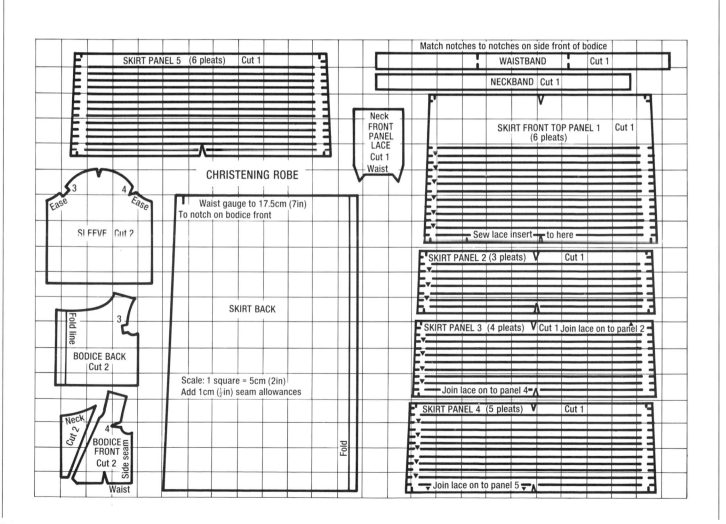

CHRISTENING ROBE

SKIRT PANEL 5 (6 pleats)    Cut 1

SLEEVE   Cut 2

BODICE BACK Cut 2

Fold line

Neck Cut 2

BODICE FRONT Cut 2

Waist

Waist gauge to 17.5cm (7in) To notch on bodice front

SKIRT BACK

Scale: 1 square = 5cm (2in)
Add 1cm (½in) seam allowances

Fold

Match notches to notches on side front of bodice

WAISTBAND    Cut 1

NECKBAND   Cut 1

Neck FRONT PANEL LACE Cut 1 Waist

SKIRT FRONT TOP PANEL 1    Cut 1
(6 pleats)

Sew lace insert — to here

SKIRT PANEL 2 (3 pleats)    Cut 1

SKIRT PANEL 3 (4 pleats)    Cut 1 Join lace on to panel 2

Join lace on to panel 4

SKIRT PANEL 4 (5 pleats)    Cut 1

Join lace on to panel 5

**7** Finish the skirt bottom by catching the lace at the bottom of the skirt to the lace on the corner of the front panel.

**8** Sew two parallel rows of gathering stitches along the top of the skirt leaving 1cm (½in) free at either side of the centre back seam.

## Bodice

**1** With right sides facing and inserting the scalloped lace between them, sew the front side panels to the triangular panels.

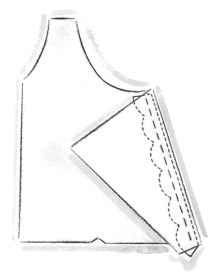

**2** With right sides facing, sew centre front panel to triangular panels; neaten and press.

**3** With right sides facing, sew front to back at the shoulder and side seams.

**4** Neaten the centre back opening by turning back 5mm (¼in), stitching, then turning back 1.5cm (⅝in) to fold line, and stitching down.

**5** Sew a line of running stitches around the skirt waist to gather it. Gather the skirt waist until it measures 56cm (22½in). Note that the skirt panel with its tucks and lace sits like an apron on the front of the robe and therefore the side seams of the bodice do not match the side seams of the skirt.

**6** With right sides facing, sew the waistband on to the bodice waist, matching the notches to the side fronts. Sew the other side of the waistband, still with right sides facing, to the skirt waist, checking that the notches on the waistband match the side seams.

**7** Sew bias binding on to the wrong side of the bodice along the same line as you sewed the waistband. Press down.

**8** Using a hemming stitch, sew the other side of the bias binding to the wrong side of the skirt waist. This is a channel through which to thread ribbon to tighten the bodice around the baby. Finish the edges of the channel by hand.

## Neck and Sleeves

**1** With right sides facing, sew the neckband on to the neck of the bodice.

**2** Sandwich the 1.5cm (⅝in) wide fine lace between the other side of the neckband and the bias binding. Sew into place. Sew the other side of the bias binding as you did on the waistband, forming a channel. Sew into place.

**3** With right sides facing, sew some of the 4cm (1½in) wide lace around the armholes ensuring that it faces towards the main body of the fabric.

**4** With right sides facing, sew the underarm seams on the sleeves. Gather the top of each sleeve, and sew into the armhole, with right sides facing. Turn up the cuff to neaten and sew on fine lace.

**5** Insert ribbon into neck and waist channels. You need approximately 1.85m (2yd) at the waist and 1m (40in) at the neck. Secure at the centre of both neck and waist with a few stitches through all thicknesses.

# CHRISTENING PIN CUSHIONS

*These Christening pin cushions are decorative and pretty and make an unusual gift. The main part of the design is traditionally made out of pin heads, but pins are sometimes interspersed with beads or old pieces of lace and narrow ribbon. Never let your baby or small child play with them as the pins can easily come out. These are keepsakes, to be treasured, perhaps to become family heirlooms.*

## MATERIALS

15cm (6in) silk, satin or a fine cotton

15cm (6in) lining fabric

sawdust or bran

small scale grid paper

thin tissue paper

rust-proof pins

108cm (43in) of 1cm (½in) wide lace

pieces of old lace (optional)

## MAKING UP

*Use 1cm (½in) seam allowances throughout.*

1 When choosing your fabrics, pale colours such as cream, white or beige look best. Keep the lining equally pale and select a closely woven fabric which will keep its shape well.

2 Cut 2 pieces of lining and 2 pieces of top fabric each measuring 12 x 15cm (5 x 6in).

3 Make the pad by sewing together the lining pieces, right sides facing, around three and a half sides. Turn right sides out and pack full with filling. Close the gap by oversewing.

4 Make the cushion cover as for the lining but take a fraction more seam allowance to give a really tight fit.

5 Work out your design on the grid paper - each square is the equivalent of a pin. The design could incorporate the baby's name, date of birth and parents' names.

6 Place the tissue paper over your design and trace it through. Place it on to the cushion and pin the design through the paper on to the cushion. Remove the paper: this is a slow and fiddly job.

7 Sew the lace by hand round the edge of the cushion and dot the lace with pins. If you have some old lace, use this too with a combination of pins to achieve a pleasing design.

# CHRISTMAS STOCKINGS

*These unusual stockings are made using a reverse appliqué technique, whereby the top fabric is cut away to reveal the fabric below. Make them in a large size to hang on the end of your child's bed or in smaller sizes to fill with inexpensive gifts for when unexpected visitors arrive at Christmas. The same pattern in miniature can be padded and decorated with sequins as a Christmas tree decoration.*

## MATERIALS

*For each Stocking*

squared paper with a 5cm (2in) grid

3 pieces of fabric each measuring 27 x 36cm (10½ x 14in) (1 plain, 1 patterned, 1 lining)

another piece of lining measuring 27 x 41cm (10½ x 16in)

embroidery threads

embroidery needle

2m (6½yd) of 13mm (½in) wide bias binding in a contrast colour

*Plus*

white and pink scraps of fabric for angel boot

beads for reverse appliqué boot

## MAKING UP

### The Angel Boot

1 Draw the pattern given to the right on the squared paper.

2 Cut out four boot shapes, one from each piece of fabric but for the second and longer piece of lining, lengthen the top of the boot by 5cm (2in).

3 Pin the top two layers (plain and patterned fabrics) together, wrong sides facing, and then baste as close to the edge as possible.

4 Cut an angel shape from white cloth. Pin her on to the front of the boot, turn under the edges and sew into place with embroidery thread using stab stitches. Repeat with pink fabric for her face. Work her hair in french knots and embroider arms, hands, wings and a halo.

5 With basting thread, mark out a border of squares at the outside top of the boot so that the tops of the squares are 4cm (1½in) down. Using very sharp, pointed embroidery scissors, cut away the top layer of fabric inside the basting stitches and then turn under the raw edges to reveal the fabric below. Sew with contrasting thread and stab stitches to neaten. Remove the basting.

6 Place the stitched boot on to the lining with the additional 5cm (2in) top (right side

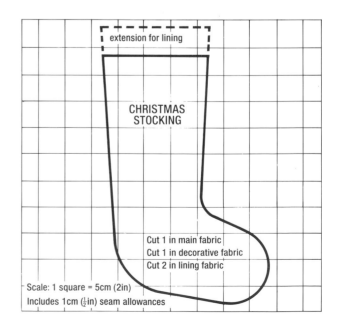

extension for lining

CHRISTMAS STOCKING

Cut 1 in main fabric
Cut 1 in decorative fabric
Cut 2 in lining fabric

Scale: 1 square = 5cm (2in)
Includes 1cm (½in) seam allowances

down) and then place these three layers on to the second lining, right side up. Pin the four layers together. Turn down the top of the lining over the front and fold under 1cm (½in) to neaten. Stitch in place with contrasting embroidery thread. Baste the four boots together as close to the edge as possible, leaving an opening at the top.

7 Sew bias binding round the edge of the boot leaving a loop at the top back and using stab stitches worked in embroidery thread.

## The Reverse Appliqué Boot

1 Make as above, but instead of an appliqué angel, make reverse appliqué circles (see page 78 for details of the reverse appliqué technique).

2 Embroider spiders and stars on to the main fabric. Add beads to the spiders to decorate.

# PAINTED PLATES

*These plates make nice mementoes or gifts for the birth of a baby or a Christening, or just make a change from pictures to hang on the wall.*

*There are many kinds of ceramic paints which can be painted on to glazed (these include water- and solvent-based paints) and unglazed china (the latter are then kiln fired). As paint specifications change constantly it is important to check the manufacturer's instructions when buying ceramic paints. Many shouldn't be used where they will come into contact with food or drink. Paints for glazed china are air dried and should only be washed by hand in the gentlest of mild washing-up liquid. As well as ceramic paints, you could use glass paints on ceramics. These are translucent and look like boiled sweets when used on glass.*

## BEGINNER'S TIPS

**1** Before starting, always have plenty of greaseproof paper or newspaper around on which to place the finished articles.

**2** Always make sure the item to be painted is clean and free of grease. Wash it in warm soapy water or clean it with white spirit before you begin.

**3** Make sure you have sufficient white spirit to wash brushes and dilute paint. You will need jam jars and lids for mixing.

**4** Keep at least two non-fluffy cloths beside you. Dampen one with white spirit to rub out mistakes. Keep the other dry to rub off any smears left by the damp one.

**5** Never overload the brush with paint unless you want to drip blobs of paint as part of the pattern.

## MATERIALS

Chinagraph pencil

glass paints

white ceramic paint

artist's brushes (various sizes)

jars and saucers for mixing

masking tape

white spirit

clear ceramic varnish (optional)

## PAINTING THE PLATES

**1** Either copy freehand the angel featured opposite or trace the outline and make a template. Use this to draw round on to the plate using the Chinagraph pencil.

**2** Mix the glass paints with white to give soft pearlized colours and then paint on to the plate using a fine brush (opposite, left). If you want to mask a part of your design while adding some details, use masking tape.

**3** Add the details around the rim (opposite, right). Here we first painted the edge of the rim with blue and decorated it with alternating dots of pale blue and pink. We then added blue stars after painting the angel.

**4** When the paint is dry leave the plate for at least 24 hours. A coat of clear ceramic varnish will help to protect the design but this isn't strictly necessary.

# CROSS STITCH SAMPLER

*In the past, samplers were very much part of every young girl's education. They were pieces of fabric upon which sewing skills were practised. The design here incorporates many different motifs, an alphabet and numbers. By following the alphabet you can write your own name or that of a new baby. Use the numbers to sew in a date or a different year. We have used 19 colours in this design but you may wish to use a more limited colour palette.*

## MATERIALS

36 x 30cm (14 x 11½in) 11-count cross stitch fabric in cream

basting thread in a contrast colour

embroidery frame

1 x DMC stranded cotton skein in each of the colours featured in the key opposite

size 26 tapestry needle

31 x 24cm (12 x 9½in) stiff piece of cardboard

pins

button thread

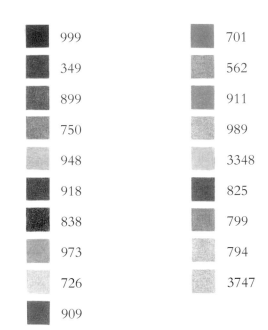

| | | | |
|---|---|---|---|
| ■ | 999 | ■ | 701 |
| ■ | 349 | ■ | 562 |
| ■ | 899 | ■ | 911 |
| ■ | 750 | ■ | 989 |
| ■ | 948 | ■ | 3348 |
| ■ | 918 | ■ | 825 |
| ■ | 838 | ■ | 799 |
| ■ | 973 | ■ | 794 |
| ■ | 726 | ■ | 3747 |
| ■ | 909 | | |

## MAKING UP

1 Mark the centre of the canvas with large basting stitches and fix the canvas into an embroidery frame to keep it taut. Move the fabric along as you work each area of the design.

2 Starting at the centre of the canvas, work the design from the chart using two strands of the embroidery thread. Work the design in cross stitch throughout remembering that one square on the chart represents one cross stitch. The top of each

stitch should slant in the same direction as all the rest. It is usual to work each stitch from bottom left to top right.

3 When the design is finished press gently on the back and mount it on the card. To do this, place the canvas over the card so that the design is central. Pin the tapestry to the board to keep it tight while you lace the back with button thread. Remove pins and then mount the whole in a frame.

# STOCKISTS

All canvas and embroidery thread:
DMC Creative World Ltd
Pullman Road
Wigston
Leicestershire
LE18 2DY

Fabric dyes:
Dylon International Ltd
Worsley Bridge Road
Lower Sydenham
London SE26 5HD

Fabric pens and Fimo:
Inscribe
Borden
Hants

Ceramic, glass and fabric paints:
Pebeo
Philip and Tacey Ltd
Andover
Hants
SP10 5BA

Sheets and quilt covers:
Dorma
PO Box 7
Lees Street
Swinton
Manchester
M27 2DD

Damask fabric:
Unit 10
Sullivan Enterprise Centre
Sullivan Road
London SW6 3DJ

Coloured Papers:
Pelikan UK
Newcombe Way
Orton Southgate
Peterborough
PE2 OUJ

# ACKNOWLEDGMENTS

The author would like to thank the following contributors:

Mrs B Bawden (for the knitted cardigan and beret)

Esther Burt (for the cross stitch sampler)

Petra Boase, 26 Sistova Road, London SW12 9QS (for the painted plates, sleeping bag, moses basket lining, crib quilt, painted cot, painted toy box and chair, and the nappy stacker)

Vicky Brooks, 45 Brownsville Rd, Heaton Moor, Stockport, Cheshire SK4 4PU (for the Christmas stockings, decorated night dresses, Princess and the pea wall hanging, animal mobile, and the travel seat)

Karen Trifit, 237 South Lambeth Road, London SW8 1XR (for the bathmat and mitts, bathrobe, painting smocks, playmat/catchpatch and the rag doll pyjamas case)

The author and publishers would also like to thank Louisa Hallstrom, Emeka Iwowo, Clare Joy, Fredrick Morton-Hooper, Alice Moxley, Robert Nicholson and Georgia Skupinski for modelling so beautifully.